TO THOSE WHO SERVE

A PRACTICAL DEVOTIONAL

Griffin Templeton

WESTBOW
PRESS®
A DIVISION OF THOMAS NELSON
& ZONDERVAN

WestBow Press books may be ordered through booksellers or by contacting:

WestBow Press
A Division of Thomas Nelson & Zondervan
1663 Liberty Drive
Bloomington, IN 47403
www.westbowpress.com
844-714-3454

ISBN: 978-1-6642-4958-5 (sc)
ISBN: 978-1-6642-4957-8 (hc)
ISBN: 978-1-6642-4959-2 (e)

Library of Congress Control Number: 2021923187

Print information available on the last page.

WestBow Press rev. date: 12/3/2021

To all those who have, are, or will lay their lives on the line for the safety and security of the United States of America whether in the military, local, state, or federal law enforcement. Thank you.

PREFACE

My purpose in writing this book is not to condemn or judge the actions taken by any of the individuals who have undertaken the noble profession of law enforcement. Nor is it to criticize the citizens of this country for the stance they take on law enforcement or the views they possess. My goal is merely to shed true light into the life of the law enforcement officer and to all those who serve, to offer perspective into the profession, and to provide encouragement and confidence for the brave ones who put their lives on the line every day.

My hope is that this book will be a guide and a resource to those in the field, providing solid answers to some of life's toughest questions. It should challenge you in ways that make you uncomfortable. It should cause you to try things outside of your comfort zone and make you perhaps think in ways you have yet to so far. I can attest it did the same for me as I was writing. In these moments, we have the opportunity to grow, if we are willing to step out in faith. If you attempt even some of what I am advocating here, you will likely feel unsure, awkward, or even silly. Rest assured that you are in good company.

This book is ultimately intended to be read more like a devotional and less like a novel. What I mean is that each chapter requires a bit of reflecting and meditating. Specifically, each chapter concludes with a list of application questions to think through. While you may be tempted to simply read the questions and continue to the next chapter, I would ask that you not do so. If you do, you will undoubtedly miss out on those precious benefits I believe the book can provide and for which I was prompted to write in the first place. Therefore, I ask you to take time to truly think upon the reality and the meaning behind each chapter, using the questions to self-reflect and encourage personal growth.

ACKNOWLEDGMENT

To my wife, your constant support throughout the writing process has made this opportunity not only possible but achievable. Thank you for your love and unending encouragement.

AUTHOR'S NOTE

Throughout this devotional, I refer to law enforcement as the primary audience; however, this audience can be interchanged for the military or other fields of service you may find yourself or loved ones called to.

"But now the righteousness of God has been manifested apart from the law, although the Law and the Prophets bear witness to it-the righteousness of God through faith in Jesus Christ for all who believe. For there is no distinction: for all have sinned and fall short of the glory of God, and are justified by his grace as a gift, through the redemption that is in Christ Jesus, whom God put forth as a propitiation by his blood, to be received by faith. This was to show God's righteousness, because in his divine forbearance he had passed over former sins. It was to show his righteousness at the present time, so that he might be just and the justifier of the one who has faith in Jesus."

—Romans 3:21–26

CHAPTER 1

How We Speak

In law enforcement, there is a great deal of what is often referred to as "police jargon." By that, I refer to the use of ten codes, shortened phrases, and abbreviated titles. Language can be specific to a certain agency or region and can even vary within the same county limits (sheriff's office vs. police department). One thing is consistent with the use of language in law enforcement, however: cursing. Despite departmental policies that prohibit cursing as a means of professionalism in the workplace and our field, we pass it off as just part of being in law enforcement.

I want to challenge this excuse for one simple reason: Jesus condemns it.

Now many of you may be tempted to immediately put the book down at this point, thinking the author may be out of touch with reality or simply too rigid and pharisaical to continue reading. I would ask you to continue for the very reason you are urged to put the book down. Change is uncomfortable, but it can produce in us the very effect we most need and desire.

Ephesians 4:29 tells us, "Let no corrupting talk come out of your mouths, but only such as is good for building up, as fits the occasion, that it may give grace to those who hear."

This is a particularly difficult truth to swallow for those in law enforcement. In the profession, you are surrounded by colleagues who make it easier for you to let a curse word slip here or there. Cursing is just as common as eating, drinking, and sleeping. It seems to run rampant. Cursing is often intermingled with joking. This topic will be discussed more at length in the next chapter. For those who do seem to cringe upon hearing God's name being profaned or a flurry of f-bombs flowing from a colleague, the typical response is simply to let it pass. This is due to the lack of courage to speak up or the lack of will to care to respond. Or it could be that you are overwhelmed by the situation and do not know altogether what to do.

This is not an opportunity to judge colleagues or to call them out for inappropriate language. This is merely a dialogue to open perspective to the reality of what you encounter every day and a chance at self-reflection on how you perform in this area. The enemy, that is, Satan, would elect to convince you to pass off foul language as a part of the job and something to just get used to. Do not allow yourself to become comfortable with it.

Often we encounter suspects and individuals in the field who cannot seem to form sentences without the use of multiple curse words. Yet I do not believe this should grant us the liberty to use similar language in an effort to build rapport. Treat people with respect and honor God in both word and speech.

You may again be tempted to put this book down at this point and claim it doesn't apply to you or that it is too judgmental, legalistic, or disconnected from real society. I am sure, however, that you would agree something has to change between law enforcement and society. I believe the most profound and effective change is going to have to come from within, from you. So I pray you would press on and grant me the opportunity to perhaps open your eyes to a greater reality while you serve the citizens of the United States of America.

My Story

I grew up in a law enforcement family with both my father and grandfather having been local law enforcement officers. I understood the value of sacrifice, integrity, and hard work from a young age. When I was a kid, I remember my mother always telling me I was only allowed to say the words she used.

She would ask me, "Have you ever heard me curse?"

The answer was, "Of course no." My mother only ever spoke loving words.

She would then say, "Well then, you aren't allowed to curse either."

This household rule only applied to what my mother said. One day after school when I was in third grade, I thought I might get by with a word I had heard my father use a few days prior when he had become upset about something at work. This was a bad idea, especially in the presence of my mother and father. I received a mouthful of soap as my punishment, much like that in *A Christmas Story*. In that moment, I was reminded that I was permitted to use only the language that my mother used. This taught both my father and me a valuable lesson.

As I grew older, I developed a typical pattern of using speech in my daily life that was certainly not God-honoring. I am not proud of it, but it is part of what the Lord rescued me from. I would do so when I became angry, but it also infiltrated casual conversation. It wasn't until I came to faith in Christ that my mindset was changed. I was in college at the time and was surrounded by a small group of college-aged men, like myself, who challenged me with the words of scripture and caused me to rethink the habits I had formed. Coming to faith in Christ brought with it a new set of desires, desires to glorify God in the things I did and the words I said.

On Duty

Again, my purpose in this chapter is not for you to hear this information and call out fellow officers for their cursing at work. If you have taken that from the chapter, then forgive me. That was not my aim. My desire is for you to challenge yourself, to compare your beliefs about language to what the Bible says about it. Language is important. Language must matter to you because it matters to God.

Would you talk the way you do at work if you were out at a family birthday lunch or gathering around the Thanksgiving dinner table with all your closest relatives? For some, the answer may still be yes. To take it a step further, what if you were in the presence of Christ? In His very presence, would you really use the language you use when interacting in the workplace in front of the Son of God? Well, for believers in Christ, the reality is simple. You are every moment. Romans 8:9 tells us, "You, however, are not in the flesh but in the Spirit, if in fact the Spirit of God dwells in you. Anyone who does not have the Spirit of Christ does not belong to him."

4

Application

1. How can you speak at work in a way that honors Christ?
2. Are there changes you need to make when it comes to language, either on or off the job?
3. What steps can you take to minimize your use of curse words?
4. How does the role of the church/community group factor into helping you achieve these goals?

Prayer

Pray that the Lord would open your eyes to the reality of your use of language. It is sometimes difficult to see things objectively when it pertains to ourselves. Thus, we need a new set of eyes. My prayer is that God may grant us the grace to speak with wisdom, kindness, and discernment as we seek to point others to Christ in everything we say and do.

CHAPTER 2

We're Only Joking

I find the topic of joking to be one of particular significance, although it does not receive the attention it deserves. I believe the root cause is found in the DNA of law enforcement officers. Law enforcement officers are strong and courageous and, if honest, can also be quite prideful. Yes, if we are honest with ourselves, we all, at our core, struggle with pride.

Note: This chapter is not focused on personal pride, but pride severely affects our ability to discern how appropriate or inappropriate our joking can be. Telling jokes is common in all professions but is perhaps more highly concentrated in law enforcement. This is namely due to the weightiness of what we do, what we see, and what we are exposed to on a daily basis.

Not many individuals would be able to witness the types of crimes we are forced to investigate. We do so without question and then proceed on with our lives as if it were just another day at the office. So how do we deal with it? One of the most common coping mechanisms we use is joking. The saying "there is a little truth behind every joke" could not be closer to the truth. We make lighthearted jokes about what we see so that we do not have to deal with the gravity and horror of what we have truly witnessed.

Now, I want to be clear: I am not saying that joking in and of itself is wrong, and I am not here to condemn all joking in the workplace. I just cannot find a justification for making jokes at the expense of others or making jokes that are ill-timed and manifested as a result of another's tragedy. Our need to deal with horrific tragedies should not grant us immunity to say whatever we wish. Yet again, many of you may be reading this and decide to put the book down at this point for fear that I am encroaching on territory of which I have no jurisdiction. I would ask you to pause before doing so. Let us allow Christ to be our authority here.

Jesus reminds us in Matthew 12:36, "I tell you, on the day of judgment people will give account for every careless word they speak." Then Ephesians 5:4 says, "Let there be no filthiness nor foolish talk nor crude joking, which are out of place, but instead let there be thanksgiving." So how can we rightly understand joking in the context of what we do? Christ alone can do the heart-changing work that brings about new affections. Further, He creates a strong distaste for what does not please the heart of God. Let us be bold in standing for Christ against crude joking, for it does not please the heart of God.

My Story

Growing up, I had the privilege of playing on high school basketball teams that competed for state championships year after year. We were talented and possessed a great deal of skill as a team, but we lacked one major component that would have set us apart: unity. My teammates and I bickered and made fun of one another nearly every chance we got. We picked on each other in the classroom and on the court, often even challenging each other to fights at practice. Some may view this as competitiveness, which, in the right context, can certainly be advantageous. In our case, it was not. Our competition amongst one another often overpowered our competition against our opponents. This all stemmed from our joking.

If we were truly honest with ourselves, our joking tore our team apart. As teenage boys, we joked about the normal topics, but sadly even our own teammates' abilities to perform on the court were not spared. I attempted to refrain from engaging in this behavior, but I too was guilty of chiming in or offering encouragement. We overlooked how hurtful the jokes were and how detrimental it was to our ability to build camaraderie. We passed everything off with a "just kidding" or "I'm just playing," but "I'm just playing" doesn't seem to remove the sting after telling him he cost us the game. We never won a state championship despite having the talent to do so every year.

On Duty

What is there to do for the rookie officer attempting to get acclimated to a new department and make a good impression with the rest of his squad? Is there anything really wrong with going along with the joke? He can offer a few mellow laughs without compromising who he is right? The way I see things, he has a choice. We all have a choice.

We are bombarded with a multitude of alternatives from the world, daily enticing us to renounce our faith, and to rebel against what we know to be right and true.

As officers, we took an oath to defend and to protect, and we did the same when we surrendered our lives to Christ Jesus. We took an oath to be imitators of Christ, to be ministers of reconciliation (2 Corinthians 5:18–20). He calls us to stand firm in our convictions. Therefore, let us do so, even at the expense of becoming the butt of the joke.

Perhaps you are thinking this book is too spiritual for you or if you are not yet a follower of Christ Jesus, this book may not be for you. I pray that you hang with me. Perhaps you will change your mind about Jesus or at least find some helpful application on the job.

Application

1. Are there better alternatives to joking as a means of dealing with the weight of your work?
2. What are the available resources to learn about effective ways of coping with the tragedies you see and investigate?
3. Am I a willing participant or a casual spectator when it comes to crude joking?
4. How might God be calling you to respond to what you have read about in this chapter?

Prayer

Pray that God would allow you to see the role you may have played in the participation or witness of inappropriate joking. Pray that the Lord would grant you the courage to take a stand for Christ against ridicule and "just kiddings." If the Lord has yet to make this topic important to you, pray desperately that he would press upon your heart its significance.

CHAPTER 3

Stay in the Fight

Y ou are surrounded by voices within your ranks and the public at large reminding you that now is the most difficult time in history to be in law enforcement. This may very well be the case. A day no longer exists in which we are able to turn on the television without hearing of a brother or sister being killed in the line of duty. You are torn by the tragedy. You seek to honor their leadership, heroism, and sacrifice. You mourn for their families and vow to learn more, train harder, and do everything in your power to protect those you hold most dear.

The challenges you face as a law enforcement officer seem to be at an all-time high. You recognize there are dangers at every turn, and as a result, you remain in a constant state of alertness. Many of you struggle to turn off the survival mindset, even after the shift ends. You bring it home with you, and sometimes it causes you to push away from others, family and friends included. Your instincts serve you well as a protector, but they also weigh on you. The effects your job can have on you are endless. To call it stress only scratches the surface. Many of you deal with depression, anxiety disorders, and post-traumatic stress disorder (PTSD). Being the strong person you are, you do not feel you can let anyone else in. You can handle it on your own, or so you try to convince yourself. At this point, you reach the danger zone.

Some of the highest rates of suicide are found amongst law enforcement officers and the military. This is not news to those of you who pay attention. You are taught it almost every year during annual in-service training. In fact, the suicide rates are much higher than the rates at which officers are killed. So why don't you spend as much time and effort learning about ways to combat depression and anxiety? You are afraid to be vulnerable. You cannot talk about your feelings because that simply is not what those like you do or you think it makes you look weak. You know exactly what it means to stay in the fight on the job. But do you know how to do so after you go home?

If you consult scripture here, the apostle Paul takes a different look at the fight. In his letter to Timothy, Paul calls Timothy to "fight the good fight of the faith" (1 Timothy 6:12). Paul has just warned Timothy to flee from the love of money, the root of all kinds of evils (1 Timothy 6:10). Paul is urging Timothy to view his life as a fight for his faith, a war being waged over the fate of his soul. He encourages Timothy to press on, to stay in the fight, the fight of faith. As followers of Christ, we are also called to remain engaged in this spiritual battle throughout our lifetime.

> For the love of money is a root of all kinds of evils. It is through this craving that some have wandered away from the faith and pierced themselves with

many pangs. But as for you, O man of God, flee these things. Pursue righteousness, godliness, faith, love, steadfastness, gentleness. Fight the good fight of the faith. Take hold of the eternal life to which you were called and about which you made the good confession in the presence of many witnesses. (1 Timothy 6:10–12)

On Duty

We know that the dangers of depression and suicide among law enforcement officers are an epidemic, but what can we do? I am not arguing we all need to huddle in a circle around a campfire and confess our insecurities and feelings (although perhaps an agency may adopt this idea). I do, however, think it is vital to begin cultivating climates that encourage discussion around this topic. Smaller groups tend to allow for more openness and minimize the fear of speaking on sensitive topics.

Regularly scheduled meetings to discuss the struggles and stresses of the job are a great place to start. I personally find it more beneficial to have this group consist of friends outside of law enforcement. Now I can already hear the objections formulating in your minds. They cannot understand exactly what we are going through, right? No, they may not be able to resonate with every detail of our jobs, but I think we will be surprised at how healthy and healing it is to share with those outside our ranks. I cannot overemphasize how vital it is to have friends outside of law enforcement. Perhaps a chapter dedicated to this topic is warranted, but the point is to get away from the job when you are not on duty. If all of your friends are in law enforcement, then you undoubtedly speak mainly about the job.

I hope this is already understood, but in case I have been too vague up to this point, this is a group with an established trust. This is a group of trusted friends, family, or church members. They have our best interest and we theirs. Ask around at your local church, even if you aren't a member, and you will more than likely find that these groups not only exist but are already meeting regularly. Don't sit on the sidelines because it is easy. Get involved. Get in the fight.

Benjamin's Story (Tennessee)

From early on in my law enforcement career, I knew I had both a passion and a knack for working narcotics investigations. I was fortunate enough that my agency allowed me to narrow my focus to working strictly on drug cases. In one of my first investigations, I initiated a case on an individual who had been selling small amounts of methamphetamine throughout a specific county. As part of the investigation, we had made several undercover purchases of methamphetamine from the suspect.

Approximately one year later, I was preparing the case to go before the grand jury to indict the individual. I decided that, before I did so, it would be beneficial to go and meet with him, to give him an opportunity to provide information about his supplier. I was singularly focused on getting the individual to flip on his source. This was always a goal I kept in the back of my mind in all of my cases because it allowed me to go after a bigger fish.

I went into the interview thinking I would accomplish the same thing I was usually able to. You can imagine my surprise when I met with him and learned that he had recently given his life to Jesus Christ and had completed a very long and grueling recovery program.

I have had people say this to me before during interviews, but this was different. This individual had truly and completely turned his life around. Not only was he no longer involved in the drug trade, but he was currently serving as an advocate for recovery.

During that interview, I pressed him hard to flip on his source to work off his pending charges, and this caused me to ask myself a difficult question. Why do I do this job? I learned a valuable lesson that day that working in law enforcement and for me, specifically narcotics, is not about the stats, seizures, or turning every case into a big conspiracy. It is, most importantly, about the people. Our job is to get bad people off the street and, if given the chance, help those bad people turn their life around.

Fast-forward years later and that same individual is still an outspoken member of the recovery community in his area and living out the rest of his life as a testimony to the redeeming power of Christ and the gospel. This job is about the people.

Application

1. What changes do you need to make in your personal life to stay engaged in the spiritual fight?
2. What passages of scripture can you read and study to help you in these areas?
3. What groups can you join (and who can you partner with) to begin thinking about and discussing issues you may be facing?
4. What steps can you take now to assist others who struggle with depression and anxiety?

Prayer

Pray that the Lord would strengthen your heart and give you the courage to join a community to begin cultivating an environment of openness and trust. Pray that you would bring your anxieties to Christ and that He would give you rest (Matthew 11:28).

CHAPTER 4

Can We Please Everyone?

Y ou are a public servant, committed to protecting the citizens of your state, county, city, and country. (I don't know who all will read this.) You are constantly in a decision-making state. You possess a great deal of discretionary power in your occupation. Everyone you come into contact with has an opinion, including your supervisors. At times, the waters can become muddied, but what is the right thing to do? This is the question I want to focus on.

You recognize you cannot please everyone, but sometimes you attempt it anyway. I am speaking to those times when you are aware of what ought to be done, but you elect to do what is easiest, despite its moral or legal repercussions. Where does that leave you? What is right is not always what is easy. The easier choice in the short run may prove to be your downfall later on. Let us evaluate the decision on pleasing people with a right perspective.

I mentioned this situation being applied to your supervisors, but this is not the only arena where this problem arises. No matter the time or place you find yourself being tested with a difficult decision, you can be assured the wrong decision will be lurking close by, ready to offer its seductive incentives. The apostle Paul put it this way, "So I find it to be a law that when I want to do right, evil lies close at hand" (Romans 7:21). Paul knew the same struggle you face today but ultimately allowed the word of God to be his tie-breaker when faced with these decisions.

We all have a moral compass, given to us by our heavenly Father (Romans 2:15), which grants us the ability to discern right from wrong. Your decisions to perform the job a specific way or act in a particular manner are guided by your morality, by what you believe to be right and wrong. Sure, you are investigating the circumstances of the case, but a law enforcement officer without a strong moral framework may find it much easier to exclude exculpatory evidence in order to close a case or obtain a conviction.

I am certainly not claiming that the only way to be a great investigator is to become a Christian, nor that investigators who are not are somehow more prone to make the wrong decision. Let me be clear: this is not the case. I am simply wanting to state plainly that from the perspective of worldview, the Christian's framework is such that morality is not determined by the shifting tides of society, whose moral compass changes from one decade to the next. Ensure you know where your moral framework comes from, where you base your decisions on what is right and wrong.

The Christian believes he works for God. We find this in Colossians 3:23, "Whatever you do, work heartily, as for the Lord, and not for men." Thus, God is the ultimate authority. When the decisions on the job or in this life do seem to get tough, let us stand with Peter and the apostles who knew they must please God rather than men (Acts 5:29).

> For I do not understand my own actions. For I do not do what I want, but I do the very thing I hate. Now if I do what I do not want, I agree with the law, that it is good. So now it is no longer I who do it, but sin that dwells within me. For I know that nothing good dwells in me, that is, in my flesh. For I have the desire to do what is right, but not the ability to carry it out. For I do not do the good I want, but the evil I do not want is what I keep on doing. Now if I do what I do not want, it is no longer I who do it, but sin that dwells within me. So I find it to be a law that when I want to do right, evil lies close at hand. (Romans 7:15–21)

Logan's Story (New Jersey)

Marine Corps commanding officers (COs) are responsible for the discipline of their troops and imbued with the responsibility of enforcing the Uniform Code of Military Justice (UCMJ) at the unit level. COs can deal with violations swiftly by holding Captain's Mast and doling out nonjudicial punishment or referring the case to Summary, Special, or General Courts-Martial, depending on the severity of the alleged offense(s).

When I was a young officer, my battalion commander appointed me as the Summary Courts-Martial officer for his unit. Essentially, my job was to hear criminal cases as a battalion-level judge. It wasn't long until a young man came before me who was infamous in our unit as a known habitual offender. He had been punished on numerous occasions at Captain's Mast, and the CO made it clear that it was time to teach the Marine a lesson by elevating the current charges to the Summary Courts-Martial level, where more severe punishments (reduction in rank, forfeiture of pay, brig time, restriction to the barracks, or hard labor) were allowed.

On the day of the trial, the courtroom was packed with both officers in my chain of command and enlisted members of our unit. They were all there to see this troublemaker receive what he deserved. As a member of the unit, I knew the accused and the facts of the case. I went into the proceeding assuming it would be easy to make a decision and hand out the punishment the CO and everyone else expected.

During the course of the trial, it became obvious to me that the young Marine was not guilty of the charges the CO had levied. When it came time to render a verdict, I felt I had to balance my reputation and the future of my career against that of a guy who clearly did not care about his.

Hindsight gives me the benefit of knowing that the decision to announce the not-guilty verdict should have been an easy one. The intensity of the moment and the knowledge of my CO's expectations clouded my thinking. However, the pressure I was feeling was nothing but moral weakness on my part, and I am thankful that God gave me the courage necessary to do the right thing.

On Duty

Sometimes we hear or read on the news about corruption within police ranks. The media then grabs hold of the story and blasts it from the most powerful loudspeaker atop the highest peak they can. But how did it happen? What drove the officer to make the decision they did? Was it pressure from a superior or perhaps something subtle that grew until it could no longer be ignored?

The latter is often the devil's strategy against us as believers. He uses seemingly harmless sins to cause us to eventually do unspeakable things, things we would never believe ourselves or our partners to be capable of doing. This is how most corruption begins. Visualize the armed robber who has successfully robbed five banks in a major metropolitan area. He did not start robbing banks overnight. He began with smaller crimes such as shoplifting or petty larceny. The same is true when we rebel against what we know in our hearts to be right and instead pursue our own selfish desires. The devil uses small compromises every day to ruin marriages, families, and careers. Do not let him win.

Application

1. What small compromises have you been making in your life?
2. What are the challenges you face when trying to make the right decisions?
3. What steps can you take to help change your desires to please God rather than men? (Acts 5:29)
4. Which spiritual disciplines (prayer, Bible study, scripture memorization, etc.) can you put into practice in order to avoid the small compromises in your faith?

Prayer

Pray that God would protect your heart from small compromises of faith and strengthen you for the battle of pleasing God rather than men. Pray you would rely on the word of God as your ultimate authority in determining right and wrong. May the God who is capable of all things be with you as you engage in the daily fight against the schemes of the evil one to draw you away from God and from making the right decisions.

CHAPTER 5

Discrimination: Are You Guilty?

Of course! You are guilty of discrimination, and so am I, but first allow me the chance to explain before you toss this book aside. I believe we, that is, every human being on the planet, are guilty of discrimination, however, not of the type of discrimination the media and political arena are quick to accuse the law enforcement profession of.

We are being told continually that law enforcement officers on the whole are guilty of discrimination. The reality is that there is a fundamental misunderstanding of discrimination. When the statement is made, the intended result is that people will conclude that law enforcement officers are unfair and immoral individuals who, more often than not, make bad decisions.

I neither agree with the accusation nor the conclusion. First, the accusation is flawed. We all discriminate every single day of our lives. When we are at the ice cream parlor and choose mint chocolate chip instead of vanilla, we are discriminating. When we are at the car dealership and we choose the Ford Mustang rather than the Dodge Challenger, we are discriminating. We are discriminating against the vanilla flavor we did not choose and the Challenger we decided not to buy.

Discrimination alone is not a bad thing. It is a crucial aspect of our capitalistic society. Discrimination becomes evil and undeniably wrong when we discriminate solely on the basis of an individual's race, for example. Initiating a traffic stop on a Hispanic individual solely on the basis of race would be the kind of discrimination officers are so often accused of. This type of discrimination is absolutely wrong, and almost every law enforcement officer in America would agree.

As I write this chapter, I recognize that mentioning the word "race" in our society may cause a myriad of emotions to flow in. You as a law enforcement officer, unlike many others, must treat everyone with respect and value. Every single human life has value because every human being was created in the image of God (Genesis 1:27). This means that every single individual you come into contact with has been deemed valuable by the creator of the universe. This truth should shape our thought process at the beginning of each day or prior to each shift.

However, this does not mean that you treat every individual the exact same way. This point cannot be overemphasized. This is a fundamental error many in our society continue to make. For example, you do not approach an individual who has committed several consecutive murders the same you would a thirteen-year-old who stole a pack of chewing gum. This is, of course, an extreme example, but it serves to drive the point home. Each individual should still be treated with overall respect and professionalism, but the approach is and should be drastically different.

The Federal Bureau of Investigation (FBI) has conducted numerous inquiries into these accusations and has concluded that less than 1 percent of law enforcement officers are actually guilty of this type of racial discrimination. Have you seen these statistics on the news? Probably not. Do not worry. The truth does not get diminished even when surrounded by thousands of ill-informed louder voices. Discrimination is necessary for everyone—yes, everyone—to live and thrive in society. "So God created man in his own image, in the image of God he created him; male and female he created them" (Genesis 1:27).

Alison's Story (North Carolina)

Make room for empathy. Lessons about being compassionate and considerate happened nearly every day in my childhood home. This was how we survived. As a clueless young black girl—I think I was eight as I recall this time in my life—I did not view myself or my family as poor, and I did not feel any shame about how we grew up until I reached high school. Food insecurity in my community was normal, as were the roaches, rats, and occasional homework by candlelight at night because the power had been turned off again. As a naïve eight-year-old child whose entire world belonged here, I believed everyone experienced these same struggles because this is what I saw. My friends and I still played together and visited each

27

other's homes as though the struggle to determine who had food did not exist.

As I stated previously, I felt no shame or embarrassment about these struggles at this point in my life. Our family did not own a car ever; we walked everywhere. I remember being excited to walk miles to the grocery store with just the possibility of picking out a favorite snack and then making our way home with what was left of the food stamp book. As I grew older and entered high school, I saw how different my home life was compared to that of a new friend I had just made at school. She was white and lived on the opposite side of town. My race and background did not seem to matter to her, just as hers did not matter to me. The fact that our ethnic and financial backgrounds were drastically different were simply insignificant facts to us. We were friends, and that was all that mattered.

We talked so often that my mom would constantly fuss about the telephone bill, despite our calls being local. This friend did not care that I was black and poor, and I did not care that she was white and appeared wealthy. We became close friends. I told her everything, and she reciprocated, even telling me how much courage she felt I had. We dreamed and cried together. Not once did she ever belittle me because of my circumstances.

One day, my hopes and dreams became quite apparent to me, as though I were waking from a deep sleep. I felt empowered to grow and do great things with my life despite my circumstances. I am not suggesting that her empathy meant she completely understood my plight or had experienced my sufferings, but her ability to listen and be a good friend meant that my life mattered to someone, someone from a totally different world.

I know that this hope for a better life was sparked by her willingness to listen with a sincere heart. Throughout my high school years, I lived in this renewed hope for a higher purpose. I have never forgotten the lesson and importance of having empathy for others. As a rookie police officer, I remember being on patrol when a fight broke out among several young girls. I arrived on the scene along with a more senior and well-known community officer. I started giving one young girl an earful about how awful and messed up she was for being out in the street at that time. Immediately I felt as though the Spirit checked me, correcting me for being out of line. This was soon followed by a similar response from the senior officer. I quickly gathered my thoughts and apologized to the girl for the way I had handled the situation. This was a lesson in empathy. When I got home that night, I said a few extra prayers to ensure God knew I was sorry for how I had acted.

I am a better person and police officer because of empathy, a sincere heart to listen with an understanding that all lives matter. My life mattered to the high school friend who inspired hope in me, and thousands of others are waiting to feel inspired to be great. Empathy is the key. Servant-leaders should always make room for empathy.

On Duty

What should you do? The answer for most of you is to simply continue doing exactly what you have been doing because you are doing the law enforcement profession proud. You don the uniform, vest, and badge every day with honor to sacrifice your life in order to keep the citizens in your jurisdiction safe. You carry yourself with the utmost professionalism. Hear it from me: You do the job incredibly well, and I want to personally say "Thank you."

The law enforcement profession is ever-changing because our

society is continually evolving, so you must too. Right? The short answer is that, in some ways, yes. Policies in your department or agency have changed over the past decade, and thus you must abide by them, but this does not mean you completely change who you are or how you do the job. Stick to what you know. It has made you the officer you are today. Hold true to your moral convictions. They have kept you alive, kept your integrity intact, and have helped you treat others with dignity and respect. You do not have to try to be the officer others are attempting to mold you to become.

Application

1. How can you examine your own heart and actions to ensure you are treating everyone with professionalism and respect?
2. How can you continue to perform your job with the increased pressure from others to conform whom you are as a law enforcement officer?
3. Are there fellow officers you work with who may struggle with professionalism regarding discrimination?
4. How can you cultivate conversations about discrimination with a fellow law enforcement officer who may struggle with professionalism?

Prayer

Pray the Lord would open your eyes to any potential for discrimination in your own heart. Pray, like David, "Search me, O God, and know my heart! Try me and know my thoughts!" (Psalm 139:23). Pray the

Lord would grant you the grace and strength to repent and change if needed. Or pray God would give you the courage to continue serving with honor despite the challenges and pressures to compromise on your convictions. May God also help you cultivate conversations with fellow officers in need of change.

CHAPTER 6

No Margin for Error

This topic is extremely timely as I pen these words in the summer of 2021, and I feel confident they will remain true whenever you happen to be reading this. What exactly do I mean when I say "no margin for error"? In most professions in the United States, performing the job incorrectly will likely result in some form of correction, verbal reprimand, or some other process of discipline. In drastic cases, one might even be fired for the mistake to perform the task, depending upon the severity of the error.

As a law enforcement officer, this is not the case. Being wrong for you may mean your life. I do not have to say much here as most law enforcement officers understand sufficiently. Making a mistake in a life-and-death situation may very well mean death. Yet this is not exactly the point of the chapter. In how many other professions is your every move, word, and action critically scrutinized? Not many, but this is the reality for the law enforcement officer in 2021.

You cannot be wrong because you cannot afford to be wrong. Being wrong means that your actions will be under examination by your supervisors, prosecutors, attorneys, media, and American citizens. While doing so, the viewers believe they are observing the entire interaction, but in reality, it is like they are watching one scene of the entire movie. This is perhaps a bit off-script, but it is often the way many people think when they are watching officer body-worn camera footage. Somehow, they believe that if it were not in the video, it did not happen.

Your actions therefore must be near-perfect, your mind incredibly sharp and focused, your body awake and prepared, your speech professional, and your heart completely ready for whatever your shift may bring. As we have seen in large numbers this year, the law enforcement officer is under the narrowest of microscopic examinations, and the possible consequences are endless. You run the risk of being terminated over the use of one single word. This has already happened to several officers. I am obviously not advocating the use of the type of language that led to the officer's termination. I am simply using the example to illustrate that you no longer have any privacy in your job. You therefore have to be aware of absolutely every second you spend on duty. "So whether you eat or drink, or whatever you do, do all to the glory of God" (1 Corinthians 10:31).

Thomas' Story (South Carolina)

As a Marine officer, I am familiar with the scrutiny of law enforcement officers, but the microscope is at a much higher magnification on today's law enforcement rather than on our military. In the late 2000s, there was a congressional recommendation that Marines carry body cameras during combat. Thankfully, the leadership of the Marine Corps shot it down for whatever reason. I'm certain there was discussion of the "Monday morning quarterback" effect that would take place, just as it has on law enforcement personnel today. Until the civilian population is inserted in the scenarios of today's military and law enforcement, they will never understand the scope of daily situations and how the margin of error and reaction for judgment is paper-thin.

Speaking to the no-defect mentality expected of military and law enforcement, I experienced this firsthand. I was in Afghanistan in 2015 conducting security missions in Kabul, a city of 4.6 million people. North Atlantic Treaty Organization (NATO) forces, including Americans, were there to "train, advise, and assist" the Afghan National Security Forces (ANSF) as they had taken control of the fight against the Taliban and similar aggressors. There were strong political opinions from the civilian population in the area, ranging from total support of NATO forces being there due to the lack of confidence in ANSF personnel to a complete disgust that NATO forces existed within Afghan borders. This was because the mentality was everything was fine until NATO showed up. At least one group was in charge with no conflict, even if it were the Taliban.

One day, we were conducting a convoy when one of our tactical vehicles was struck by a massive vehicle-borne improvised explosive device (VBIED) right in the middle of the city. The vehicle's occupants were dazed but alive. A few Afghans were killed or injured as well. A crowd of Afghan civilians quickly surrounded the strike zone, and the area was complete chaos almost immediately. As the convoy members exited their vehicles to set a security perimeter and tend to the impact vehicle's occupants, the crowd became even more chaotic with yelling, crying, and running in all directions. Suddenly a man emerged from the crowd with a large knife and charged the convoy leader just outside of one of the vehicles. Fortunately the convoy leader's flak jacket SAPI plate stopped the blade on the initial strike, and the convoy leader was able to apprehend the man, take the knife, and push away the man, who then fled back into the crowd. As the crowd reacted to this, mostly to help, the dozens of approaching civilians were deemed a potential threat by a member of the convoy, and he fired several warning shots directly at a civilian vehicle demolished in the blast. The crowd moved away from the convoy and quickly disbursed.

After the convoy cleared out of the area and the damaged vehicle was immediately recovered, word started to spread around the world that a VBIED had struck an American convoy and severely damaged a vehicle. Unfortunately, the *New York Times* printed an account of the incident by a supposed Afghan journalist who was nearby that made several claims. First, he stated that the Americans had fired into the crowd and killed several Afghan civilians. Next, he stated that the crowd was shouting "death to America" while cursing the convoy members. Finally, he never mentioned the knife-wielding man attacking the convoy leader. The article also stated, "American department of defense members did not respond to questions from the *New York Times*." This is normal practice as no Department of Defense spokesman will comment on events until a thorough investigation is complete. However, a perfectly worded statement made the reader detect guilt from members of the Department of Defense.

After the story printed, American forces were given a huge black eye. To win a counterinsurgency, military forces do not focus on eliminating all of the enemy, but instead turning the populace against the enemy to drive out supporters of their cause and to choke them of resources. This article severely took us in the wrong direction, and in the months to follow, we were all walking on eggshells among the Afghans. Relationships that took years to cultivate were damaged. A few weeks later, the Taliban conducted a complex attack on another NATO base and killed an American servicemember, to which they claimed was a response to the "NATO attack on Afghan civilians."

Did the members of the convoy make an egregious error? No. Could they have performed better after a review of the situation? Probably. However, the perceived actions caused enough damage to our mission that it was as if it were true.

On Duty

I am not claiming to possess a foolproof plan for avoiding mistakes on duty. That is impossible. The goal is to offer a few options to help minimize the number of mistakes made during a shift and to ensure more officers return home in good standing with their departments and the citizens they have taken an oath to protect.

The common denominator here is the mind of the law enforcement officer. If I can get just one law enforcement officer to employ one of these suggestions prior to each day, then this chapter has accomplished its purpose. The first is to pray before every shift, investigative stop, interview, call for service, search warrant, court appearance, and day. The power of prayer is an amazing gift. When you focus on speaking to the creator of the universe in prayer, it has a way of humbling you and centering your mind around what is truly important. The meaninglessness of distraction seems to fall away. This, in turn, will help you get much clearer on the objective you have set out upon.

Another helpful option is to make a list of the five most important things in your life right now. You can make this list before your shift or whenever you have downtime. Then actually write the list down in your own handwriting. Putting these priorities on paper will help make it more real. It is okay to put the list in your phone as well, but it will have a greater impact when you see it in your own handwriting. Keep the list in a place where you can visualize it often. Keeping your priorities in order will help you avoid simple mistakes.

Last, ask yourself the question, "What's important now?" again before each shift, investigative stop, and so forth. This question will be familiar to many of you and is connected to the list of priorities from the previous paragraph. Asking yourself this question can further help you concentrate on the task at hand without being consumed by other thoughts that have no bearing on your immediate circumstances. For example, "What's important now as I am about to conduct this interview? Am I in a safe location? Is my partner with me for this interview? Am I mentally prepared for the interview?" This question can be applied to every aspect of the law enforcement officer's duties. I pray it would be helpful for you.

Application

1. Take a look at how you typically start your workday and what you do to prepare for it.
2. Pray prior to the start of each day, shift, call for service, investigative activity, and so forth.
3. Make a list of the five most important things in your life right now and keep it somewhere visible.
4. Frequently throughout the workday, ask yourself, "What's important now?"

Prayer

Pray the Lord would keep your mind sharp prior to every shift, investigative stop, call for service, interview, court appearance, search warrant, and day. Ask God to help you remain focused for the entirety of your shift. Ask the Lord to give you the strength to serve and protect your community with dignity. Pray the protector God would watch over you and your families as you place your life on the line every day.

CHAPTER 7

Purpose

———————

M y hope is for this chapter to cause you to examine your heart and motives for being a law enforcement officer. I pray this chapter would cut deep to the heart of the law enforcement officer. Often I think that, for many, the law enforcement profession has lost the pride and honor it once held. I am not speaking of the societal perception, but within the law enforcement community itself.

Law enforcement is among the noblest of professions. It calls people from all walks of life to join an elite group of individuals who have collectively taken an oath to protect and defend the constitution of the United States of America and the citizens who live and work here. Law enforcement officers are protectors of freedom and keepers of the peace and are willing to go into the darkest of places to ensure that light can continue to shine throughout our country.

Law enforcement officers should not take this oath lightly. They should not join this profession for prestige or the authority. It should be a clear calling upon the heart. It is not a job to be taken without serious consideration and contemplation. The training alone is enough to deter most. The job can be dangerous, costly, and extremely difficult. It can be emotionally draining, physically taxing, and mentally exhausting. This can, in turn, produce a great many negative effects on the law enforcement officer's health, family life, and financial position.

Why do you continue to do it? This is the question I want you to ask yourself. The law enforcement profession needs people who want to take the job because they know it is what they are called to do because they know they would be unsatisfied and unfulfilled in any other profession. Law enforcement is hurting for numbers, and it needs more people who put others before themselves, who are willing to put their own lives on the line in the place of others. If I am describing you, then you know you are in the right place or you know where you are supposed to be. "When justice is done, it is a joy to the righteous but terror to evildoers" (Proverbs 21:15).

David's Story (Virginia)

Why do we do it? I grew up in the late 1970s and early 1980s watching police shows like *CHiPs, Hawaii 5-0, Miami Vice, Dragnet, Hill Street Blues,* and others of that time. As a young kid, I understood that these TV shows had a common theme: no one works alone, and they all battled some type of wrongdoing to help those in need. All I knew was that I wanted to be part of that, plus who wouldn't have wanted that CHiPs helmet and mirror sunglasses as you drove that motorcycle.

Many of us have similar stories as to why we chose this calling, this profession, this lifestyle. Mine is no different than most. I had the need, drive, and aspiration to do something important where I could serve God as well as be part of a profession that provided for my family and made them proud, a profession that is respected and noble despite the present-day negativity. Serving God is one of the most important principles of the Christian faith. "For even the Son of Man came not to be served but to serve, and to give his life as a ransom for many" (Mark 10:45).

I have been fortunate to have a career that not only provided for my family but also gave me the satisfaction that I was doing something that mattered. For me, becoming a police officer was a dream come true. The longer we stay in this job, we are all prone to get complacent and grow tired of the department politics, the media, and the negative public attitudes, but for one second, think back to when you first got the call or letter informing you that you have been offered employment with your agency. Better yet, think of the feeling when you first received your badge and were sworn in. Did your spouse, parent, child, or police chief pin that badge on you?

When this job gets to you or you feel you are growing complacent, think back to that day and try to look back on how far you have come and how many lives you have impacted, for better or worse. Again, my story is no different. I started as a young, twenty-three-year-old uniformed police officer. I loved chases, arresting drug dealers and robbers, helping stranded motorists change a tire, and giving kids a high five. Later I was promoted to detective and continued working on catching drug dealers to rid my community of the poison. I later pursued federal law enforcement to do the same work, but at a national and international level.

I have worked cases from local street corner dealers to cartel members attempting to set up distribution hubs in our communities. I have also seen the exploitation of humans: women, men, and children exploited for labor and/or sex by people who seek only greed. I have worked several human trafficking investigations, and in so many cases, the victims themselves did not even identify as victims. Many were reluctant to accept housing, food, or job placement assistance, much less cooperate in an investigation against their trafficker. But for those few who did accept, some went on to live successful lives.

One that stays with me is the story of "Claire," a woman lured into a relationship by a "Romeo pimp," only to be sexually exploited by her "husband." The exploitation occurred weekly and lasted for thirteen years. The husband did not work during that time and used Claire as the source of income and their children as bargaining chips, routinely telling her that he would harm them if she did not comply. The husband also branded Claire's neck with a tattoo of his name, a common tactic of traffickers.

God set our paths to intersect on December 23. The husband had severely beaten Claire and had broken three of her ribs because she did not want to go on a "date" with a repeat "client." Regardless of the injury, the husband drove Claire to the date and promised to take her to the hospital after the date. The client immediately saw she was in medical distress and did the right thing by getting her to a hospital to receive medical attention. While in the hospital, she revealed her story to an aunt living across the country, and that aunt called the National Human Trafficking Hotline to report the story. I subsequently received the email lead from the trafficking center. Instead of waiting to assign it to an investigator after the holidays, I sent it to one of our best investigators, and we immediately began an investigation that lasted six months and identified several past victims.

At the end of the investigation, we rescued Claire and her three children, placed her in a shelter, and provided her assistance to work. She attended community college for her associate's degree, and she was finally able to become an independent person. Her husband was prosecuted and pled guilty in federal court, resulting in a thirty-year sentence. Claire is a survivor and now uses her experience to help others. Sadly, these success stories are few and far between, but when you ask why I do this job, it is because of Claire, and I will always look back on the good I was able to do.

Remember the feeling of getting that badge? Well, the small victories, although they may be few, brought about the feeling of fulfillment that you were doing what you were meant to do. Like many of you, we could sit here and share war stories, but I challenge you to think of why you do it. It is not just because it's a job that pays the bills; it is a calling for something greater than yourself.

"And I heard the voice of the Lord saying, 'Whom shall I send, and who will go for us?' Then I said, 'Here am I! Send me'" (Isaiah 6:8).

On Duty

I believe it is extremely beneficial in life to constantly and consistently reflect on what is most important. This gives perspective to what we are doing and to how we are living. To ask yourself daily, weekly, or monthly "What is most important?" will be an extremely helpful exercise on evaluating what is most important to you. It will further help you identify the areas in your life that may require change.

Jesus said in Matthew 6:21, "For where your treasure is, there your heart will be also." If you are like me, you sometimes find yourself saying certain things are really important to you. Yet, if you examined where you spend your time, money, and effort, you would quickly realize your statement does not measure up. If we apply the principle of Matthew 6, it can help to expose areas of our lives that require change.

Where do you as the law enforcement officer find your treasure? Much of our time is spent at work. This is certainly not to say that your treasure is your job, but it does help to illustrate the point that you should enjoy or derive purpose out of what you spend so much of your time doing.

Application

1. Think of the things you would say that are most important to you.
2. Compare those things from point one to Matthew 6:21. What do you find?
3. If you find significant disparity, think about why that might be and what might be causing it.
4. Develop strategies as to how you might spend more time and energy on the things you believe are truly most important to you. Ask yourself what will be most important in the long run.

Prayer

Before you begin to apply these things, ask that God would bring to light the most important things to you. Pray that these things would be brought into view of how you spend all your time, energy, effort, and money. Ask that God might expose the inconsistencies about your perceived treasure and where your treasure currently lies. Finally, pray that God would bring into focus where your treasure should truly be and allow your heart to follow.

CHAPTER 8

Returning Home

I want to focus this chapter on the condition in which you return home. Law enforcement officers spend most of the day alternating between various levels of stress and alertness. For most law enforcement officers, home is not only where the heart is, but where you are able to rest. This is the place you can return to a resting heart rate, a place where you can destress and truly relax your minds and bodies. This is assuming that you do not return home to a chaotic household. I am of course joking here.

As important as it is for you to be able to destress and relax, it is equally important for you to be present for your spouse and children. You do not have the luxury of checking out and not being present at home. If this is your default, I urge you to make amends and change this soon. Too many marriages have ended as a result of law enforcement officers not being able to deal with coming home.

So what happens when law enforcement officers come home

that leads to quarreling, anger, and loneliness? The law enforcement officer finds solace in solitude. It is not that you enjoy being lonely, but that you yearn for the mental rest and rejuvenation it supplies. This state of detachment, however good it feels temporarily, is not entirely helpful or healthy. In the end, it always produces negative results.

Officers look forward to this time, but unfortunately it means they are not communicating with their spouse. Further, it means they are isolating from their children. Even the best law enforcement officers only have so much energy left to give to their spouses and children. This may seem like something everyone deals with after work, but it is distinctly different and severely enhanced for the law enforcement officer. This is so for the many reasons I have explained in earlier chapters regarding the many stressors and dangers associated with the job.

> God is our refuge and strength, a very present help in trouble. Therefore, we will not fear though the earth gives way, though the mountains be moved into the heart of the sea, though its waters roar and foam, though the mountains tremble at its swelling. The Lord of hosts is with us; the God of Jacob is our fortress. Be still, and know that I am God. I will be exalted among the nations, I will be exalted in the earth! (Psalm 46:1–3, 7, 10)

Max's Story (Illinois)

Over the past twenty-plus years, I've been fortunate to maintain two career paths, one in law enforcement and one in the military.

As a veteran of several combat deployments and numerous law enforcement operations, the "refit," or return home, is an often-neglected phase of our chosen profession. For me, the comradery of a cohesive group committed to a focused effort has always been the draw of these careers. The training to support the mission, execution of the plan, and candid after-action analysis condition us to be better than we were, with the earned knowledge of lessons learned.

During my first combat tour, I was able to regularly maintain communication with my spouse. The words "I want to know everything" were uttered, and I thought I could share some of the non-sensitive events that occurred throughout. After a few weeks, the words "I don't want to know everything" were also uttered. At the time, it was a slap in the face because I didn't see the events in the same light as my spouse. She viewed them as potentially life-ending events for me and, ultimately, her. It took her the better part of a year to tell me that. In the interim, I called home less and less, creating other issues that took counseling and time to sort out.

After that first tour, I was reminded by the unit chaplain that our spouse's frame of reference on our exciting day was much different than ours. As professionals in these disciplines, we take pride in saving lives, providing security, and "winning" the day. To our spouses, our daily activities could potentially be earth-shattering to their world. I had never really viewed it that way (rather selfishly). This helped me to frame my communications with my spouse and children in a more palatable manner.

Additionally, involving my family with the teams I worked with helped to diminish their fear of danger to me, as they could sense the commitment to the team. The guys would reference events, and my family would listen intently and then later state, "You never told us that story." They were learning that I was protecting them from wild thoughts and worries. As a daily routine, it was not uncommon for my children to rush to the door and bombard me with their daily activities as soon as I got home. Unfortunately I didn't respond well to that either. After all, I had just made it home another day, safe and sound. If I could just get fifteen minutes to decompress, then I could be Daddy. It didn't take long, and soon my children wouldn't come to greet me when I arrived home anymore. Then it hit me, "I'm being selfish again." I had my priorities out of order. I was selfless to the nation, to my profession, but why not my family? Arguably, shouldn't they get the first and best version of me?

It took some time, tears, and genuine talks to reset the priorities. Fortunately, with effort, open communications, and attention, we were able to grow from the events. While some information is best kept in the appropriate circles, involve your family in your work life. The exposures greatly enhance understanding and build confidence that you will make it home to them.

On Duty

It is vitally important for the spouse of the law enforcement officer to understand what goes through the mind of their husband/wife when they return home from work in order to respond accordingly. Thus, it is crucial for you, the officer, to communicate exactly what goes through your mind when you end your shift and return home. It is important to communicate these things as early as possible. The longer you wait to have the conversation, the more difficult it may be.

It is not acceptable to simply pass off that your spouse will not understand. It is your responsibility to communicate in such a way that they know exactly how you are feeling. Now, this conversation does not need to happen every single day or even week. It might be beneficial to have the conversation monthly, simply as a reminder. The more your spouse understands what you are going through, the better they can respond to you. This serves to alleviate the tension of feeling like you must be a ball of energy when you return home. Every day may be different; therefore, it may be necessary to send a text to let your spouse know you had a tough day. The more aware you can make your spouse, the easier it will be on you.

Application

1. Plan a specific time to have a conversation with your spouse/ friend about everything that goes through your mind when you end your shift and return home.
2. Think through specific things you want your spouse/friend to know.
3. Brainstorm ways your spouse/friend can best respond to you.
4. Have the conversation and trust the Lord would be with you both as you talk and think through these things.

Prayer

Pray the Lord would give you the courage to be vulnerable and have a difficult conversation with your spouse, friend, or whoever is closest to you and can be an advocate for you. Ask that God would reveal who this person might be for you if you are not married. Trust that God would provide the ultimate rest you need and would be your refuge from the pressures and stresses you encounter daily.

CHAPTER 9

The Need for Accountability

I spoke in the last chapter about the need for you to speak with your spouse about what goes through your mind when you return home. This prompted me to want to address the same issue for those who are single. For you, it is entirely different. You have the sole responsibility of looking out for yourself. You have the freedom to grab fast food on the way home, have a cold beer, and sit in front of the television for hours until you fall asleep.

Many would argue this is their best method of decompressing after work, and it is not entirely bad, but it could be much better for one simple reason. When you do this, you are isolating, and even though that show or movie may distract you or make you laugh, it does not discuss what you saw the previous shift, and it cannot take the place of a friend, spouse, family member, pastor, or counselor who can listen to you and encourage you.

Most of us are type-A personalities, which means we find it extremely difficult to open up to other people and be vulnerable about what is going on in our lives. This is a protective mechanism that has served you well so far, or so you tell yourself. The fact is that police officers are at the highest rate of suicide among all other professions (addiction center.com). In 2018, 172 officers lost their lives to suicide. That is almost twice the number of line-of-duty deaths from 2018 (106).[2, 3] In 2019, there were a record 228 law enforcement officer suicides. This number is almost triple that of line-of-duty deaths in 2019 (89).[4] Not only are these statistics sad, but they will continue to be amplified when you factor in a pandemic and the current views among some about law enforcement in the country.

Thus, it is of vital importance for you to have someone in your life that you can regularly speak to about how you feel, what is going on, and when things seem as though they are spinning out of control.

Terry's Story (North Carolina)

Truth in law enforcement is as important as providing safety and protection to the people being served. Historically, telling the truth, regardless of the consequences, has been critical in law enforcement. Less than ten years ago, I retired from law enforcement after serving the same city for thirty years. My father, who served in local law enforcement prior to me, taught me the invaluable lesson that a law enforcement officer lives in a glass house.

Those wise words spoken so many years ago are just as applicable in today's world. We must not forget that law enforcement personnel are human, like everyone else, and will make bad decisions or mistakes in the performance of their duties. Due to the discretion and power that law enforcement officers are given, particularly the responsibility of taking away a citizen's freedom, they will always be held to a higher standard than any other profession.

Truth is defined as that which is true or in accordance with fact or reality. It often seems, however, that we are living in a society that says truth is whatever a person believes to be true. Some say there is no such thing as absolute truth. God's word, documented in the Holy Bible, says different. Jesus said that he is the way, the truth, and the life and that no one comes to God the Father except through him. Knowing and having a relationship with Jesus allows us access to the Father. Accepting Jesus as Lord and Savior changes us from the inside out. As each day passes, we strive to be more and more like Jesus. Everything about Jesus is true: what he thought, what he said, and what he did.

Law enforcement must stand on the truth when it comes to hiring standards, internal investigations, serving people and businesses, criminal investigations, collection of evidence, swearing and serving warrants, testifying in court, and relationship with media. Anything less leads to a spiral effect causing distrust, lost friendships, loss of respect, and hatred to the point of physical harm. The public's perception of law enforcement has caused changes in the judicial system, media, and police agencies as well. Law enforcement is spending considerable amounts of time and money attempting to adapt to these rapidly evolving changes. The rate of hiring and firing of personnel seems to be at an all-time high, in addition to the number of officers being charged criminally.

Today's law enforcement is forced to capture almost everything they do on video to prove or back up what was done. If not, the public has been made to believe that they must be hiding something or trying to lie about what really happened. Thirty short years ago, if a law enforcement officer swore to tell the truth in a court of law, whatever they testified to, along with physical evidence collected, was enough to gain a conviction.

How, in such a relatively short period of time, have things concerning truth changed so much? Could it be related to the lack of accountability? Several things that have contributed to this change include access to the internet, smart phones, and the rise of social media. What people are constantly exposed to will create and modify physical behavior. For law enforcement officers, certain influences are out of your control. Simply focus on the only thing you can control, you. Do the right thing. Speak words of kindness and gentleness. Seek after someone who will be willing to mentor, love, encourage, and hold you accountable. Failure to do so will potentially cost you something someday, or it may cost you everything.

I once knew an excellent young officer who was smart, trustworthy, professional, and confident in their abilities. The officer soon started down the road of bad decision-making and soon became ensnared by the temptations of this world. These bad decisions led to a double lifestyle that would eventually claim the officer's career and marriage. Lying about an assignment resulted in an internal investigation, which presented the officer with the choice to tell the truth about what happened. When confronted with the choices made, this officer lied rather than tell the truth. The agency lost a great officer that day, but the officer lost much more. The statement given to me by my father about the glass house was true, and regretfully for this officer, the glass house had come crashing down.

On Duty

I do not wish to sound like a broken record here to so many things you have undoubtedly heard already, not just from me, but from countless trainings your department may have given you. While the access to resources and advocacy groups from a department is wonderful, they are also filled with well-meaning strangers. I have no doubt that the people who are part of such great organizations are kind and caring people, but to the law enforcement officer, they are still strangers, and most do not trust that what is said in confidence won't get reported back to their department.

For those who do use and have used such resources, I applaud you. I think more officers should. There are confidentiality privileges that hold the power of law with most mental health counselors, so this is a safe bet. However, this can still be a hurdle for many, in that it may feel as though they have to admit, in some way, that they need mental health help.

I am a huge believer in having someone in your life who knows you better than anyone, someone you share true fears, challenges, and details about your life, someone you do not keep things close to the vest with. This is someone you can trust with the deepest things you hold on to. While decompressing at home on your couch with a beer and burger in front of the television after work may sound awesome, it is simply not the best thing for you and your future. You need someone in your life who can routinely check in with you, not just a phone call or a text message, but a one-on-one, sit-down conversation over coffee on a Saturday morning.

O LORD, you have searched me and known me! You know when I sit down and when I rise up; you discern my thoughts from afar. You search out my path and my lying down and are acquainted with all my ways. Even before a word is on my tongue, behold, O LORD, you know it altogether ... Search me, O God, and know my heart! Try me and know my thoughts! And see if there be any grievous way in me, and lead me in the way everlasting! (Psalm 139:1–4, 23–24)

Application

1. Find the person in your life you can trust most with the most intimate details. If you do not already have someone who fits this description, then begin to cultivate this type of relationship.
2. Tell them how important it is for you to have someone like them who you can speak about the stresses and struggles of your life as a law enforcement officer.
3. Ask them if they are willing to be that person for you (whatever you wish to call that person, i.e., accountability partner, etc.)
4. Begin to meet with this individual regularly face-to-face at least once per month.

Prayer

Pray that God would give you the strength to be open about the stress and struggle you face as a law enforcement officer and the willingness to communicate honestly about your feelings. Ask that the Lord would provide the right individual to have those conversations with and that God would make it a priority in your mind to set time aside regularly to meet with them. I pray and ask that God would provide you all the tools you need to be successful in this fight. I pray that the Lord would search you according to Psalm 139 and lead you in the way everlasting.

CHAPTER 10

Protect Your Mind

Perhaps it is best to begin this chapter by stating what exactly I am calling you to protect your mind from, to put it simply, the bad thoughts. I do not wish to limit what could be included here, but this may encompass fears, doubts, family issues, relationship problems, and finances, just to name a few. Sin is the root of all of these issues. Let me explain what I mean.

Sin is the root of fear and doubt in not seeing God as the sovereign King of the universe, ruling and reigning over every situation. Sin is behind many different kinds of family and relational issues, expressed in multiple different ways. Sometimes they are exposed in a small fight with an angry response at others. They lead to deeper issues such as infidelity. Sin is at the core of financial problems as well when you fail to be a good steward of the finances God has provided. We are simply managers of what God entrusts to us financially. The Bible tells us in Proverbs 22:7, "the borrower is the slave of the lender." Where you find doubt and fear, you will find sin lurking.

"Be sober-minded; be watchful. Your adversary the devil prowls around like a roaring lion, seeking someone to devour" (1 Peter 5:8).

These problems can build up in such a way that they reach a point in which we can no longer block them out. They can begin to pervade our thoughts in such a way as to keep us from focusing on what is most important in the moment. I do not need to repeat myself, but this can be a major problem for the law enforcement officer. How, therefore, can you keep these bad thoughts out? I must admit here that I have set up a false premise. The reality is that you cannot. You must bring these things out. You must talk about them. You must confess them. You must pray about them if you wish to overcome them.

Michelle's Story (North Carolina)

When I began my law enforcement career, I was young and naïve and had just graduated college. I was twenty-four years old and had studied criminal justice for the past several years. I believed I had a sufficient understanding of what I would be facing in undertaking a career as a law enforcement professional. I had been raised in a Christian home by parents who were strict but thought it more beneficial to expose me to the harsh realities of the world rather than shelter me from them. I understood that there were bad people in this world and that they did bad things. Little did I know, however, that I would come face-to-face with 100 percent pure evil.

In my first six years as a law enforcement officer, I was exposed to a teenage son viciously killing his mother and father, a trusted soccer coach sexually assaulting several of his soccer players, and multiple police officers killed by the very people they took an oath to serve and protect. A few years ago, I began noticing myself becoming impatient, callous, and cold to people I interacted with, whether witnesses, victims, or even other law enforcement officers. I had been warned that this happened to all law enforcement officers, that I would soon become like this after time and after witnessing true horrors. I too started to repeat that all-too-familiar comment, "I hate people." I found myself saying harsh and negative things about drug addicts, thieves, predators, and murderers.

This was not who I wanted to be or how I wanted to live, and the Lord soon convicted my heart. To state it simply, I lost focus. I lost focus on the truer and greater reality. The Jesus that I have given my life to and who saved me from an eternity of separation from Him loves these people. I need to love these people too. The greater reality is that we are called to be like Christ. We are called to commune and love those who are considered unlovable. God sent His Son Jesus to die for our sins! He loves us, regardless of the things we have done. That is a miraculous and overwhelming love. If we had to be perfect to be saved, then we would all spend an eternity apart from Christ.

Although we are in this profession and we witness a great deal of terrible things, it does not mean that we can categorize people as unsavable or unlovable. We are all broken people, desperate and in need of a relationship with Jesus Christ.

"for all have sinned and fall short of the glory of God, and all are justified freely by his grace through the redemption that came by Christ Jesus" (Romans 3:23–24). "But God demonstrates his own love for us in this: While we were still sinners, Christ died for us" (Romans 5:8).

On Duty

Again, I want to reemphasize that you cannot keep secret things hidden. They will eventually come out. Perhaps you are thinking to yourself here that you have it all together and that the things you hold onto are really not as bad as other people. I would issue a warning that if you are comparing your righteousness to others, you need to act quickly. You are beginning to justify the things you are doing, and this will only make it more detrimental in the end. "For nothing is hidden that will not be made manifest, nor is anything secret that will not be made known and come to light" (Luke 8:17).

Much like the previous chapter, you must utilize the people in your life to talk about these tough things. These may be the most difficult conversations you will ever have and the most fruitful. If there is something you need to make known, I urge you to do so, no matter how dirty, sinful, or hard it may be. When you do so, I anticipate you will begin to see these difficulties transform before your very eyes, and I pray this would be the case. It will, in turn, begin to clear your mind and your conscience. The bad thoughts will then no longer haunt you on the job or enter into your mind to distract you from your duties.

Application

1. Think and pray that the Lord would help you identify the bad thoughts as identified in this chapter.
2. Write these things down. This may help you see (perhaps for the first time) that you need help to resolve these things.

66

3. Identify the right person in your life to have these conversations with. You may need to have multiple conversations with different people.
4. Have the conversations and share these things. Pray for the Lord's help and courage for you before you do.

Prayer

I pray God would give you the courage to examine your own heart and mind to discover your struggles and the issues that plague and distract you. We all have different struggles, and I hope you will be willing to do this hard heart work. Ask that God would expose these things to you and then pray for forgiveness when He does. Pray then that the Lord would grant you the strength to share these things with those whom you need to.

CHAPTER 11

Who Do You Serve?

When thinking about the topic of whom you serve as law enforcement officers, the answer seems to be very simple and straightforward. Obviously law enforcement officers are sworn to protect and serve the citizens of the United States and to defend the Constitution of the United States of America. In today's day and age, these things appear to get slightly distorted, whether by media portrayal or human perception. The fact that more obstacles appear to stand against these truths only serves to brighten their reality.

For example, if you asked most law enforcement officers whether they believe they are supported by the public, you may or may not be alarmed to hear that many do not feel the citizens they protect support the work they do. The point of this chapter is not to denigrate the citizens of this country or the media for not being more supportive. Rather, for law enforcement officers, it is a call to lift your eyes and, in so doing, hopefully lift your perspective as well.

You are ultimately called to serve only one. This remains true for every human being in the world, not just law enforcement, but this book is primarily concerned with those who serve. You are called to serve God. Yes, it is true. You serve the people of this country, but you serve God primarily. I mean that, in how you serve, you are serving the people as though you are serving the Lord because, in an ultimate sense, you are.

> As each has received a gift, use it to serve one another, as good stewards of God's varied grace: whoever speaks, as one who speaks oracles of God; whoever serves, as one who serves by the strength that God supplies-in order that in everything God may be glorified through Jesus Christ. To him belong glory and dominion forever and ever. Amen. (1 Peter 4:10–11)

On Duty

Thus far in the devotional, I have spoken a great deal about the perspective of the law enforcement officer. Regarding this chapter, your perspective can only shift when your focus does. If you focus on what you perceive to be only negative opinions, this will shape the way you view society and, more importantly, will have a significantly negative effect on the way you perform your job.

I want to shift the perspective on who you are serving first and foremost. At the beginning of each day, focus on the one you are called to serve primarily. The Lord alone can elevate your perspective and help to keep you from eventually sinking into the depths of self-deprecation and despair, where you reach the point at which you begin to believe that what you do no longer matters, and this is profoundly untrue.

Application

1. Be honest with yourself about who you truly serve and how often you think about this concept prior to and during work.
2. Spend time evaluating what you believe about how society perceives you as a law enforcement officer. (This may look different for the law enforcement officer depending on location.)
3. If you find yourself feeling negative about the public's perception of you, speak to someone you trust about it. Ask them their opinion of you as a law enforcement officer and law enforcement officers in general.
4. Spend time with the Lord asking God to help you view your calling in terms of 1 Peter 4 and not the way the world may.

Prayer

Pray the Lord would alleviate the current feelings you have for those you are called to serve and protect. Ask that God would help you to see a greater calling to serve Him and seek to glorify God in all you do, both on and off the job. Pray the Lord would create a fresh perspective for you to view society. Ask that the Lord might grant you peace if you look around and see none. Finally, pray that God might allow you to become a light in the neighborhood, cities, states, and nation you are called to serve and protect.

CHAPTER 12

The Legacy You Leave

I want to shift the focus a bit here to an incredibly important topic, yet often neglected until it is too late to make significant changes: retirement. Sure, people in law enforcement talk about retirement all the time. There is at least one individual in every department who has all the details about how best to retire and where to put your money. Then almost everyone else is singularly focused on time. Most can even tell you the months and days they have remaining until they are eligible to retire.

I am certainly an advocate of knowing both the time remaining until you are eligible and what retirement vehicle is best to invest your money. One of the most critical steps to ensure you are able to retire is to actually invest. Most people do not even invest their money until it is too late to see a significant return.

Now that you are actually going to invest your money, let's discuss where to do so. Your city, county, state, or federal government will almost all have a 401(k) plan available to you. I highly recommend utilizing this as your primary investment plan. However, and I want to be clear here, do not leave your money inside their career cycle fund plans. They all undoubtedly have different names for them, but they are almost all the same. There is an aggressive plan, a conservative plan, and something neutral in the middle. I, along with countless others, have fallen victim to these plans and left my money in far longer than I should have. It was at a time when I was ignorant about investing and I listened to everyone else's opinion without taking the time to get educated.

This is my next piece of advice. Hire an investment professional and ask them to teach you about investing. It is willfully ignorant to continue to invest your money in something you do not understand. Once you have some baseline knowledge, ask them to take a look at your current investment portfolio and make recommended changes. This is exactly what I did, and within a few months, I saw significant growth. Again, I want to reemphasize the point. Do not continue to invest in a plan just because everyone else told you to or because it is what the government suggests. Learn for yourself and then make the most educated decision after you have obtained the knowledge necessary to do so.

On Duty

You will be amazed at the level of comfort and peace you receive from having an investment professional in your life. Most professionals, not just law enforcement, worry about when and, most importantly, if they will be financially able to retire. All these worries are solved when you have an investment professional who is there to guide you through this process and to ensure you are exactly where you need to be when you reach the point of retirement. Having these worries alleviated will make you a better law enforcement officer for the rest of your career.

The Bible speaks to this very issue in 1 Timothy 5:8, "But if anyone does not provide for his relatives, and especially for members of his household, he has denied the faith and is worse than an unbeliever." How are you able to provide for the members of your household if you do not understand or know whether you will be able to financially retire? It is crucial, therefore, that you act as soon as possible to ensure you can do so. You do not want to be staring out at retirement with one year remaining, not knowing if you are financially prepared.

Application

1. Identify your situation and look at your retirement numbers. There are two places I recommend you check out: DaveRamsey.com and ChrisHogan360.com.
2. Look for an investment professional in your area. I highly recommend again DaveRamsey.com. He and his team have vetted thousands of investment professionals, and this is a quick and easy way to find some close to you.
3. Meet with the investment professional and ask them to teach you some of the basics about investing. Ask them to take a look at your current investment portfolio and specifically where your money is invested.
4. Listen to what the investment professional has to say and then make an educated decision. Hopefully by now they have explained a bit about investing and you feel comfortable enough to take their advice.

Prayer

Pray the Lord would impress upon your heart the importance of providing for your family and the need to gain knowledge and wisdom to do so. Ask that God would put the right person in your life to help you to accomplish this. If you are facing worry or anxiety about this, pray that God would give you a peace that surpasses understanding and would grant you clarity as you navigate through this new terrain. Entrust the plan you currently have for your life to the Lord and allow the Lord to direct you.

CHAPTER 13

Retire ASAP

When most law enforcement officers speak about their retirement, they most often reference time, the time they have remaining before they are eligible to retire. Somewhere between twenty and thirty years is the total time in which most law enforcement officers find themselves serving. This is an incredibly long term of sacrifice. For this reason, I implore you to retire when you can. The country is grateful for the time you have given to keep it safe.

It is to your benefit that you retire as soon as you are eligible. Even those who love the job do not envision doing it for the rest of their lives. Most often, they do not have a plan for what to do next. Many just wish to enjoy retirement, go fishing, and travel. However, I believe there is a danger in not having a purpose in which to contribute.

We were created to work, and there is an inherent dignity associated with work.

You derive a great deal of purpose in the work you have done as a law enforcement officer. Leaving the profession to go fishing will not stimulate your mind or provide the satisfaction you need. To be clear, I certainly have nothing against fishing or hunting. These can be excellent ways to clear your mind and allow you to rest. Unless you are a professional hunter or fisherman, I highly recommend you find something else to do with your time. This is the time for your encore career, time for you to get involved in your church or charity of choice.

"There is nothing better than that all should enjoy their work, for that is their lot. Whatever your task, put yourselves into it, as done for the Lord and not for your masters" (Colossians 3:22–23).

Therefore, I desperately want you to find something else to do with your time because sitting around watching television and waiting for your next vacation will lead you into depression. Again, you were created for work, and you have already proven you have tremendous value to add. Continue with this notion and find something else to do. Perhaps it is a hobby you have always had that you thought you could make a career. Now is that time.

On Duty

It is popular among some in the profession to continue working well after they are eligible, believing they cannot afford to take the cut in pay. Yet the mistake they are making is focusing singularly on the salary figure. In nearly every circumstance, it is more beneficial financially for you to leave the job when you are eligible. You have to take into consideration all the things that you will no longer be paying into such as retirement and pension.

For example, let us say that you were retiring with a final salary of $80,000. You are obviously not taking home the full amount because of taxes, but you are also paying into a 401(k) plan, pension (usually 5 to 7 percent), Social Security (6 percent), Medicare (1.5 percent), and taxes. Taxes are often overlooked, but in most cases (and this depends on the state you reside in), you will be taxed less because you are making less money.

Here is the breakdown in North Carolina, for example, for an individual making $80,000 as final compensation: 1.82 percent of average final compensation (multiplied by) years and months of creditable service.

- $80,000 x 1.82 percent = $1,456
- $1,456 x 30 years = $43,680
- Now, let us add back in what is no longer coming out of your paycheck.
- Pension: 6 percent of $80,000 = $4,800
- Social Security: 6.2 percent = $4,960
- Medicare: 1.45 percent = $1,160
- 401(k): $19,500

Let us consider the full amount for those who are maxing out their 401(k) retirement. plans. Now, to summarize:

$43,680 + $4,800 + $4,960 + $1,160 + $19,500 =$74,100

This is 92 percent of the final compensation! You could open a lemonade stand on Saturdays to make up the remaining 8 percent.

Every state will vary, but the point remains true. It does not make financial sense to continue working after you are eligible to retire. I hope this will be helpful for you as you determine your own retirement eligibility and financial projections. No matter where you are in your career, you should start to look at and calculate your projected retirement.

Application

1. Take a look at your retirement eligibility and the time you have remaining before you are eligible.
2. Find the formula for your specific retirement plan and create a financial retirement projection plan.
3. Evaluate whether you think you will be able to financially afford to retire. Trust me. You will.
4. Start to think of possible encore career opportunities or places you wish to serve and then take steps to make them a reality.

Prayer

Pray that the Lord would help you begin to think and plan for retirement. This is wise; therefore, ask the Lord for wisdom to think through these things. Pray the Lord would help you to plan, but ultimately that God would establish your steps as you think through what to do after you retire from law enforcement. "The heart of man plans his way, but the LORD establishes his steps" (Proverbs 16:9).

CHAPTER 14

Encore

In this chapter, I want to focus on goal-setting. This is absolutely essential for the law enforcement officer because of how most generally view retirement. Law enforcement officers rush to reach the retirement mark and then do not know what to do with the rest of their lives. If you plan to retire and go on a few vacations, hunt, fish, and relax at home, I can assure you that your life will feel unfulfilling.

I do not say this lightly because I eagerly wish for a different outcome for your lives. You were created for more than consuming and enjoying life. I need to say here that I want you to take vacations. I want you to hunt and fish. I want you to be able to relax and enjoy time at home with your family. However, you were created to contribute, to give, and to make much of your life through influence and work.

Most of you have spent your life serving the communities of the United States and world, to protect its citizens and keep them safe. For that I am grateful. I just ask that you do not stop there. Do not say to yourself that you have given enough and now it is time for you to rest. I am not advocating you continue in law enforcement, just that you consider continuing to do something that stimulates your mind and your body. I would call this your encore career.

Find something you enjoy doing, something you love to do that you have always wanted to try. Then go out and give it a shot. Think about what skills you have and how you might utilize them to provide, produce, or serve. I want you to set goals to achieve this new position. Setting goals will help you to prepare as you are nearing retirement and will ensure you do not reach that mark with no idea what to do for the rest of your life.

On Duty

So how do you put this into practice? How do you begin to set goals for your future after retirement from the law enforcement profession? I think the best place to begin is with conversations with your spouse or, if single, friends or family. Sit down with someone and dream about what you would like to do together. Dream about where you would like to visit. What dream vacation would you like to go on? What charities or organizations would you like to give to? Are there people in your life that you would like to help? Perhaps there is a single mother who struggles to pay her bills every month. Is there a hobby you would like to take on: golf, hunting, or fishing?

Then think about how you wish to spend most of your time. The above-listed items are important for you to feel like you are retiring, but they will not be what fills most of your time. This is why I am advocating so strongly for you to find an encore career now before your retirement. It is important for you to do this now in order to best prepare yourself for the transition once you reach retirement.

Setting goals will help you do things like updating your résumé and getting training and certificates on skills that may be required. Start to research potential careers and document what you need to get the job. These small steps now can help to greatly reduce anxiety at retirement.

Lastly, as you begin to think through your next career and the goals you have for you and your family after retirement, think about investing in people. Take time to build meaningful, lasting relationships with people the Lord has placed in your life. It is important to be investing financially, but much more so to be investing in people. Your financial investments may last to benefit you, your children, and possibly even your grandchildren, but the investment you make in other individuals will have a much longer and lasting effect. "And these will go away into eternal punishment, but the righteous into eternal life" (Matthew 25:46).

Application

1. Start to have conversations with your spouse and dream about retirement: vacations, hobbies, giving, and encore career. Write them down.
2. Research encore career opportunities and qualifications needed to obtain the job.
3. Dust off your résumé, update it, and get training/certifications required for the job.
4. As you approach retirement, begin to reach out to potential employers, take them out to coffee, and meet to discuss future employment.

Prayer

Pray the Lord would open your eyes to how you are currently viewing your retirement and if any change in perspective is necessary. Pray God would help you to think through your encore career and steps to take to help achieve this position. Pray the Lord would help you to think about investing in people, not just finances. I ask that God would be with you as you think through these important issues.

CHAPTER 15

Focus on the Future

A s important as it is to focus on the future, and specifically on the financial aspect of retirement, I must state one point emphatically. Do not become consumed with finances and retirement. It is certainly important to focus on your future and the reason I have devoted three chapters to the topic. However, this focus on your future encompasses much more than finances, goals, and time.

I wish to offer a warning to you, one that is by no means original to me. You cannot take your treasures with you when you meet the Almighty. He will not be impressed with the size of your home, the view from your vacation home, the cost of your car, or the amount in your bank or retirement accounts. I wish to encourage you to give. Give generously to those in need. The Lord has blessed you with everything you have, for "Every good gift and every perfect gift is from above" (James 1:17).

It is important to provide for your family's future, but much more to leave a legacy of giving, a legacy that points your family to the ultimate source of all things. Leave a legacy that others will remember you for how generous you were. It is true that it is far better to give than to receive.

"Do not lay up for yourselves treasures on earth, where moth and rust destroy and where thieves break in and steal, but lay up for yourselves treasures in heaven, where neither moth nor rust destroys and where thieves do not break in and steal" (Matthew 6:19–20).

Give to the furthering of the kingdom of God. Invest in people. Invest in relationships. These investments will give you a far greater return than any other investment could. They are guaranteed to last for all eternity.

CONCLUSION

I pray that this book has been both illuminating and a source of encouragement for you. If it has been, I pray you would offer it to others, that they may perhaps be blessed by it as well.

When I was contemplating the very concept of writing this, I often questioned whether anyone would read it and whether it would help anyone. This last question was the one I thought about most often. I did not wish to simply provide remedies for societal problems. I wanted to look within to try to address deeply personal core issues, not to help you become a better version of yourself, but to point you to the only one who can satisfy our souls.

> "Thou hast made us for thyself, O Lord, and our heart
> is restless until it finds its rest in thee."
> —Saint Augustine of Hippo, Augustine, *Confessions*,
> 1.1.1.

CONTRIBUTOR'S ACKNOWLEDGMENT PAGE

I want to extend a special appreciation to all the men and women who helped write the stories in this book and for being willing to share personal anecdotes from their lives and careers. They each possess unique and qualified expertise to speak on the topics in this book, much more so than me I would like to add.

Each story was personally written by these individuals who have served in law enforcement and/or the military, from special operators to members of local, state, and federal law enforcement agencies. All names have been intentionally altered to protect their identities.

- Benjamin, Tennessee, Law Enforcement
- Logan, New Jersey, Military
- Allison, North Carolina, Law Enforcement
- Max, Illinois, Law Enforcement and Military
- Thomas, South Carolina, Military
- David, Virginia, Law Enforcement
- Terry, North Carolina, Law Enforcement
- Michelle, North Carolina, Law Enforcement

BIBLIOGRAPHY

1. "New Study Shows Police At Highest Risk For Suicide Of Any Profession," https://www.addictioncenter.com/news/2019/09/police-at-highest-risk-for-suicide-than-any-profession.

2. "Record number of US police officers died by suicide in 2019, advocacy group says," https://abcnews.go.com/Politics/record-number-us-police-officers-died-suicide-2019/story?id=68031484j; Blue H.E.L.P (nonprofit).

3. "FBI Releases 2018 Statistics on Law Enforcement Officers Killed in the Line of Duty," https://www.fbi.gov/news/pressrel/press-releases/fbi-releases-2018-statistics-on-law-enforcement-officers-killed-in-the-line-of-duty#:~:text=According%20to%20statistics%20reported%20to,51%20officers%20died%20in%20accidents.

4. "State Law Enforcement Officers," https://www.myncretirement.com/non-retirees/current-employees/benefits/leos/state.

SCRIPTURE INDEX

English Standard Version

Chapter 1

1. "Let no corrupting talk come out of your mouths, but only such as is good for building up, as fits the occasion, that it may give grace to those who hear" (Ephesians 4:29).
2. "You, however, are not in the flesh but in the Spirit, if in fact the Spirit of God dwells in you. Anyone who does not have the Spirit of Christ does not belong to him" (Romans 8:9).

Chapter 2

1. "I tell you, on the day of judgment people will give account for every careless word they speak." (Matthew 12:36)
2. "Let there be no filthiness nor foolish talk nor crude joking, which are out of place, but instead let there be thanksgiving." (Ephesians 5:4)
3. "All this is from God, who through Christ reconciled us to himself and gave us the ministry of reconciliation; that is, in Christ God was reconciling the world to himself, not counting their trespasses against them, and entrusting to us the message of reconciliation. Therefore, we are ambassadors for Christ, God

making his appeal through us. We implore you on behalf of Christ, be reconciled to God." (2 Corinthians 5:18–20)

Chapter 3

1. "For the love of money is a root of all kinds of evils. It is through this craving that some have wandered away from the faith and pierced themselves with many pangs. But as for you, O man of God, flee these things. Pursue righteousness, godliness, faith, love, steadfastness, gentleness. Fight the good fight of the faith. Take hold of the eternal life to which you were called and about which you made the good confession in the presence of many witnesses." (1 Timothy 6:10–12)
2. "Come to me, all who labor and are heavy laden, and I will give you rest." (Matthew 11:28)

Chapter 4

1. "So I find it to be a law that when I want to do right, evil lies close at hand." (Romans 7:21)
2. "They show that the work of the law is written on their hearts, while their conscience also bears witness, and their conflicting thoughts accuse or even excuse them." (Romans 2:15)
3. "Whatever you do, work heartily, as for the Lord, and not for men." (Colossians 3:23)
4. "But Peter and the apostles answered, 'We must obey God rather than men.'" (Acts 5:29)
5. "For I do not understand my own actions. For I do not do what I want, but I do the very thing I hate. Now if I do what I do not want, I agree with the law, that it is good. So now it is no longer I who do it, but sin that dwells within me. For I know that nothing

good dwells in me, that is, in my flesh. For I have the desire to do what is right, but not the ability to carry it out. For I do not do the good I want, but the evil I do not want is what I keep on doing. Now if I do what I do not want, it is no longer I who do it, but sin that dwells within me. So I find it to be a law that when I want to do right, evil lies close at hand." (Romans 7:15–21)

Chapter 5

1. "So God created man in his own image, in the image of God he created him; male and female he created them." (Genesis 1:27)
2. "Search me, O God, and know my heart! Try me and know my thoughts!" (Psalm 139:23)

Chapter 6

1. "So whether you eat or drink, or whatever you do, do all to the glory of God." (1 Corinthians 10: 31)

Chapter 7

1. "When justice is done, it is a joy to the righteous but terror to evildoers." (Proverbs 21:15)
2. "For where your treasure is, there your heart will be also." (Matthew 6:21)

Chapter 8

1. "God is our refuge and strength, a very present help in trouble. Therefore we will not fear though the earth gives way, though the mountains be moved into the heart of the sea, though the waters roar and foam, though the mountains tremble at its swelling. The

Lord of hosts is with us; the God of Jacob is our fortress. Be still, and know that I am God. I will be exalted among the nations, I will be exalted in the earth!" (Psalm 46:1–3, 7, 10)

Chapter 9

1. "O LORD, you have searched me and known me! You know when I sit down and when I rise up; you discern my thoughts from afar. You search out my path and my lying down and are acquainted with all my ways. Even before a word is on my tongue, behold, O LORD, you know it altogether. Search me, O God, and know my heart! Try me and know my thoughts! And see if there be any grievous way in me, and lead me in the way everlasting!" (Psalm 139:1–4, 23–24)

Chapter 10

1. "The rich rules over the poor, and the borrower is the slave of the lender." (Proverbs 22:7)
2. "Be sober-minded; be watchful. Your adversary the devil prowls around like a roaring lion, seeking someone to devour." (1 Peter 5:8)
3. "for all have sinned and fall short of the glory of God, and all are justified freely by his grace through the redemption that came by Christ Jesus." (Romans 3:23–24)
4. "But God demonstrates his own love for us in this: While we were still sinners, Christ died for us." (Romans 5:8)
5. "For nothing is hidden that will not be made manifest, nor is anything secret that will not be made known and come to light." (Luke 8:17)

Chapter 11

1. "But if anyone does not provide for his relatives, and especially for members of his household, he has denied the faith and is worse than an unbeliever." (1 Timothy 5:8)

Chapter 12

1. "There is nothing better than that all should enjoy their work, for that is their lot." (Ecclesiastes 3:22)
2. "Whatever your task, put yourselves into it, as done for the Lord and not for your masters." (Colossians 3:23)
3. "The heart of man plans his way, but the LORD establishes his steps." (Proverbs 16:9)

Chapter 13

1. "And these will go away into eternal punishment, but the righteous into eternal life." (Matthew 25:46).

Chapter 14

1. "As each has received a gift, use it to serve one another, as good stewards of God's varied grace: whoever speaks, as one who speaks oracles of God; whoever serves, as one who serves by the strength that God supplies-in order that in everything God may be glorified through Jesus Christ. To him belong glory and dominion forever and ever. Amen." (1 Peter 4:10–11)

Chapter 15

1. "Every good gift and every perfect gift is from above." (James 1:17)

2. "Do not lay up for yourselves treasures on earth, where moth and rust destroy and where thieves break in and steal, but lay up for yourselves treasures in heaven, where neither moth nor rust destroys and where thieves do not break in and steal." (Matthew 6:19–20)

ABOUT THE AUTHOR

Griffin Templeton earned a degree in criminology and has experience in both state and federal law enforcement as a criminal investigator. Law enforcement, military service, and the Christian faith run deep in his family roots.